Being Human

Being Human

Levi Tafari

Being Human

Text copyright© 2025 Levi Tafari
Front cover photo: Stephanie de Leng
Back cover photo: Steve Wood

ISBN 978-1-0687103-1-5

The Author has asserted his rights under the Copyright,
Designsand Patents Act 1988 to be identified as the author
of this work.

Conditions of Sale
No part of this book may be reproduced or transmitted by
any means without the permission of the publisher.

British Library Cataloguing in Publication Data.
A catalogue record for this book is available from the
British Library.

1 3 5 4 2

First Published in Great Britain
Hawkwood Books 2025
Blackpool Enterprise Centre FY4 1EW

Printed and bound in Great Britain by CPI Group (UK)

For Dave Ward

In a world and time where being kind can be rare, you have truly embodied the true meaning of being human.

You have been there from the early days of my poetic journey as a poet, not only as a mentor but a constant source of support and encouragement, but also as a valued friend.

You have opened doors, created opportunities for me. You understood my mission as an urban griot and the message I wanted to relay through my work. You elevated I, never asking for anything in return.

Your generosity, kindness and unwavering belief in my work has meant so much to me.
This book "Being Human," feels especially fitting to dedicate to you, because you have exemplified its very essence, and I am proud to call you, my friend.

With deep appreciation and respect.

Levi Tafari, May 2025

LEVI TAFARI - is a crucial, rhythmic, poetic, consciousness-raiser and 'Urban Griot' from Liverpool, England.

As a writer and performer Levi has worked locally, nationally, and internationally in Africa, the Caribbean, Europe, America, Singapore, China and Jordan. Writer-in-Residence at Charles University in Prague. Collaborated extensively with the British Council in Europe and the Far East for flagship education and arts projects *BritLit* and *Inclusion and Diversity In Education* (INDIE).

Writer-In-Residence at University of Liverpool Management School. Writer-in Residence at Liverpool Hope University Department of Education. Work with LFC Foundation on their Mental Health Programme.

Musical projects include working with Ghanaian drum and dance ensemble **Delado**, the **Liverpool Philharmonic Orchestra** and his own reggae fusion band **Ministry of Love**. Toured with **Urban Strawberry Lunch** in the UK, Europe and the Far East; and worked with jazz musician **Dennis Rollins**.

Television appearances include *Grange Hill* and *Blue Peter*. Subject of BBC TV's Everyman programme *The Road To Zion* about the Rastafarian movement in Ethiopia. Contributed poetry to Channel 4's award winning documentary, *A City Fit to Live In*.

Admitted onto the roll of **Citizen of Honour of the City of Liverpool** September 2022. Presented with a Lifetime Achievement Award by **Roots 40** at a ceremony at the Legacy Centre of Excellence, Birmingham.

A mural of Levi by artist Paul Curtis accompanied by a plaque of the poem *Shape Your Destiny* is installed on the corner of Jordan Street and Jamaica Street in Liverpool, supported by Baltic Creative.

CONTENTS

A CREATOR OF UNITY	1
IT MAKES SENSE	4
POET	6
SHIFTING	7
ANCHORED	8
LET US CELEBR8	11
LOOK WITHIN	16
WHERE DO YOU STAND	18
HUMAN RACE	19
FIGHTING FOR PEACE	22
THE WAR CONTINUES	24
A LETTER OF CONCERN	27
FALLING TEARS	29
HOPE	32
TIME	34
A CITY FIT TO LIVE IN	35
R LIVERPOOL	40
LFC POETRY IN MOTION	43

BRILLIANT BOBBY FIRMINO	46
HEARTFELT LOVE	49
BEAUTIFULLY BLISS	50
YOU MAKE MY LIFE WORTHWHILE	51
LOVE LIFE LAUGHTER	53
WHEN IT COMES TO LOVING	54
CAN YOU FEEL IT	57
MAKE THINGS HAPPEN	59
WATER	61
WE NEED A SOLUTION	62
SEFTON'S WONDEROUS WATERWAYS	65
A SYMPHONY OF COLOURS	67
BOOK	70
WILL OUR GRANDCHILDREN BE ROBOTIC?	71
IT'S WHERE WE'RE GOING	74
BEING HUMAN	76
ACKNOWLEDGEMENTS	77
NOTES	78

A CREATOR OF UNITY

My identity is a mystery
because my story is erased from history.
My genealogy is of an African ancestry
which has left a legacy for the whole of humanity.

I am crucial, rhythmic, poetic consciousness
    raiser –
an urban griot overflowing with culture.
Born in Liverpool to parents from Jamaica –
yes I'm Levi Tafari, a unity creator.

My faith is Rastafari –
    give thanks and praise unto Jah Jah.
My spiritual homeland is the land of Ethiopia.
My philosophy is one love, peace, respect
    and honour.
I display dynamic dreadlocks –
    people know me as a Rasta.

My skin is rich in melanin,
    but I am more than a colour.
I am a son, a brother, a husband and a father.
I love my family – I love them to the very core –
they are the blessing in my life,
    I couldn't ask for any more.

I celebrate my culture, I would never abuse it.
I express myself through rap, hip-hop,
    jazz and reggae music.
I am a man of the people,
    I feel and share your plight.
When it comes to revolution,
    I will stand up for my right.

I am not monolithic –
    my attributes they can be seen.
I am a qualified chef –
    I studied classical French cuisine.
I could whip you up a meal
    using a single grain of rice –
then I will get you hot and steamy
    with some Caribbean spice.

I love gracing the stage,
    my poetry is my passion –
creating rhymes, telling of the times
    in a poetic fashion.
Travelling around the world,
    this gives me inspiration –
My poetry is a reflection
    of my Rastaman vibration.

My community is precious to me,
    I embrace her spirit.
I always write with her in mind –
    this is how we do it.
Toxteth is my neighbourhood –
    it's the place where I was raised.
I deal with the drama of the ghetto,
    and I never get fazed.

So I've created a self-portrait
    of some of who I am –
a human being in love with life, I love this creation.
I stir things up creatively for the love of humanity.
I live the life I love to live,
    because I'm just being me –
a creator of unity!

IT MAKES SENSE

Can you see the THUNDER
    roaring like a BEAST?
Can you see the WIND as he drifts to the east?
Can you see your BREATH
    on a SIZZLING SUMMER DAY?
Can you see the OZONE LAYER
    as she slowly fades away?

Can you smell the SUNSHINE
    beating down on your face?
Can you smell the MUSIC
    that is gyrating your waist?
Can you smell the LIGHTNING
    zigzagging across the sky?
Can you smell the PAIN when a baby cries?

Can you hear a MANGO growing on a tree?
Can you hear the CORAL
    singing in the Caribbean Sea?
Can you hear the RAINBOW radiant and bright?
Can you hear the MOON
    as she sheds her light at night?

Can you taste the WORDS
    as they roll off your tongue?
Can you taste all the SONGS
    that you have ever sung?
Can you taste the MEMORIES
    roaming around in your head?
Can you taste the SLUMBER
    as you sleep in your bed?

Can you feel the LOVE flowing from this poem?
Can you feel the UNITY
    that this poem is showing?
Can you feel the ENERGY
    that this poem is GIVING?
If you can feel this POEM –
    you are alive and truly LIVING!!!

POET

Wordsmith motivator
Image creator
Thought provoker
Foundation shaker
Liberty taker
Imaginative troublemaker
Headline grabber
Poetic blabber
Identity retainer
History sustainer
Stage performer
Lyrical entertainer
Audience seducer
Inspirational producer
Solemn figure
Flowing river

SHIFTING

The shifting sands of a distant shore
inspired the search for life and a promise of more.
Wandering, chasing a whole new dream –
prosperity and hope in new pastures of green.

Leaving behind the life they knew so well –
the pain of leaving makes the heart ache
    and swell.
Promises to loved ones of a brighter future,
coming to terms with a whole new culture.

Decisions are made,
new foundations are laid.
The heart is obeyed
while hoping to be paid.
Decisions are made,
new foundations are laid.
The heart is obeyed
while hoping to be paid.

A loss of freedom leads to distress.
Doubts and fears breed loneliness.
Hesitant but hopeful – this is human nature.
Travel broaden horizons –
    embrace a whole new culture.

ANCHORED

Mi mother and mi father left from Jamaica –
say them moving to Britain
    where the grass is greener.
They heard that the streets were paved with gold,
but they didn't realise the land was grey and cold.
Them received an invitation
    from the British government –
the promise of residence and employment.
In this New Jerusalem
    they had hopes and dreams –
achieving all you can through ways and means.

THEY HAD FAITH INN DE COUNTRY,
    FAITH INNA DE CITY –
GRAND IDEAS THAT THE RIDE
    WOULD BE PRETTY.
LITTLE DID THEY KNOW,
    THINGS WOULD BE SO HARD –
YOU SEE THEY HAD DARK SKIN
    AND THEY CAME FROM ABROAD.

Casting their anchor as an act of faith,
holding on to their roots – this was no debate.
The foundation they laid, it was an act of trust –
unity in the community was a must.
Love, light and laughter – fond memories of home.

Blood, sweat and tears
>   now they are here on their own.
Conflict in integration creates a stumbling block
as the anchor of my people
>   remains firm in the dock.

THEY HAD FAITH INN DE COUNTRY,
>   FAITH INNA DE CITY –
GRAND IDEAS THAT THE RIDE
>   WOULD BE PRETTY.
LITTLE DID THEY KNOW,
>   THINGS WOULD BE SO HARD –
YOU SEE THEY HAD DARK SKIN
>   AND THEY CAME FROM ABROAD.

The people colonised by the British Empire
came from the Caribbean,
>   Africa and parts of Asia.
They ventured to Britain for their piece of the pie –
they had no idea it was so high up in the sky.
But they endured the experience
>   through staying power.
Through culture and religion
>   they are staying together.
They brought many gifts to the Empire –
>   now their ideas unfold.
Britain is now a multi-cultured rainbow –
>   what a sight to behold.

THEY HAD FAITH INN DE COUNTRY,
    FAITH INNA DE CITY –
GRAND IDEAS THAT THE RIDE
    WOULD BE PRETTY.
LITTLE DID THEY KNOW,
    THINGS WOULD BE SO HARD –
YOU SEE THEY HAD DARK SKIN
    AND THEY CAME FROM ABROAD.

LET US CELEBR8

WE SHOULD CELEBR8
NOT DISCRIMIN8 –
LEARN TO APPRECIATE,
DON'T PLAYER HATE –
BECAUSE THERE'S ROOM FOR YOU
AND THERE'S SPACE FOR ME,
LIVING IN THIS WORLD OF DIVERSITY –
LET'S CELEBR8 DIVERSITY.

Nature has dressed us up
in many shades of skin.
The variety of tone we display
is the result of melanin.
If you hate your neighbour
because of their skin colour,
you really hate yourself –
as we are all versions of each other.

People embrace religion,
but still they fuss and fight.
Many believe in one God,
so why on earth don't they unite?
There are many different faiths –
we have lots of beliefs,
so let's celebr8 our differences
instead of crying out in grief.

WE SHOULD CELEBR8
NOT DISCRIMIN8 –
LEARN TO APPRECIATE,
DON'T PLAYER HATE –
BECAUSE THERE'S ROOM FOR YOU
AND THERE'S SPACE FOR ME,
LIVING IN THIS WORLD OF DIVERSITY –
LET'S CELEBR8 DIVERSITY.

Battle of the sexes –
the competition is rigid and strong.
Women cry out for equality
as men treat them wrong.
Society creates roles
for the genders to define –
I know we are the yin and yang
but we could be floating on Cloud Nine.

The elders in our communities,
they still have a lot to give.
You don't reach that golden age
by being stupid –
so let's respect our elders
to lift their spirits higher,
as everyday we're getting older –
like them one day we'll all retire.

WE SHOULD CELEBR8
NOT DISCRIMIN8 –
LEARN TO APPRECIATE,
DON'T PLAYER HATE –
BECAUSE THERE'S ROOM FOR YOU
AND THERE'S SPACE FOR ME,
LIVING IN THIS WORLD OF DIVERSITY –
LET'S CELEBR8 DIVERSITY.

When it comes to sexuality,
there is true diversity.
Now-a-days sexual expression
is red hot and spicy.
Some people abstain –
others reveal different identities.
STRAIGHT, GAY, A or BISEXUAL –
which is your category?

Some people will criticise you
for the clothes that you wear.
Others will even bully you
for the colour and texture of your hair.
Whether you're short or tall,
super-size or wafer thin –
people love to judge you on your appearance
instead of exploring the person that is deep within.

WE SHOULD CELEBR8
NOT DISCRIMIN8 –
LEARN TO APPRECIATE,
DON'T PLAYER HATE –
BECAUSE THERE'S ROOM FOR YOU
AND THERE'S SPACE FOR ME,
LIVING IN THIS WORLD OF DIVERSITY –
LET'S CELEBR8 DIVERSITY.

Now disabilities they vary –
society has a long, long way to go.
People exclude disabled people
as if they are really slow.
Equal opportunities are vital
for disabled people to succeed.
your disability is not the problem –
it's the world that doesn't cater to your needs.

Refugees are really suffering –
who really knows their plight?
Refugees are fleeing persecution
in the middle of the night.
Dressed in desperation,
where do they go from here?
We all need somewhere to live –
free to live without living in fear.

WE SHOULD CELEBR8
NOT DISCRIMIN8 –
LEARN TO APPRECIATE,
DON'T PLAYER HATE –
BECAUSE THERE'S ROOM FOR YOU
AND THERE'S SPACE FOR ME,
LIVING IN THIS WORLD OF DIVERSITY –
LET'S CELEBR8 DIVERSITY.

LOOK WITHIN

They say that seeing is believing –
but that is foe,
because looks can be deceiving
as we all should know.
So don't judge a person
by the colour of their skin –
check out their heart deep within.

Now we should never judge a book by its cover,
as we only see its face and not its true nature.
Open up the book to get the full picture –
then you will reveal the book's true character.

Your heart and soul reveal your personality –
your measure, your worth,
    your essence is the key.
So, expand your mind, journey and explore –
it's not about DNA, it's your persona,
    it's your core.

Beauty runs deep –
not only in the eyes of the beholder.
It's what we see inside –
physical traits change as we grow older.
Dr. King dreamt of getting to
    the mountain top together –

it won't be achieved
    by judging each other's colour.

They say that seeing is believing –
but that is foe,
because looks can be deceiving
as we all should know.
So don't judge a person
by the colour of their skin –
check out their lifestyle,
how they are living.

WHERE DO YOU STAND

Know what you stand for, know where you stand.
Don't be a bandwagonist and follow the band.
Principals and wisdom will carry you through –
know what you stand for and to that be true.
Stand for justice, stand for peace.
Stand for equality, so life will increase.
Stand for others, be true to yourself.
Stand for life's worth, not just for material wealth.
Stand for something, stand up right.
The great Bob Marley said –
   "Don't give up the fight."
Stand for knowledge and don't just believe.
Stand for a goal you know you can achieve.
Stand against war, stand against oppression.
Stand against poverty, stand for liberation.
Stand for mental freedom, stand for who you are.
If we all stand for each other, humanity will go far.
Now a man who stands for nothing –
let's put it into context – will fall for anything,
words from brother El Shabazz aka Malcolm X.
What do I stand for? – I hear you cry.
I stand for one love, one heart, one destiny –
I stand for RASTAFARI.

HUMAN RACE

Race is a carving, carved by man
like shades of wood in a carpenter's hands;
manipulated and shaped to fit historical plans –
spreading far and wide across many lands.

People talk about the human race,
but race is a human construction.
So, when you analyse its true meaning –
race is a competition.

Today they call it modern slavery,
historically it stripped you of your identity.
Across the Atlantic Ocean,
    you were no longer free –
the race was started with intentions of inequality.

First place, second place –
some come third.
Sometimes people cheat,
which is absurd.

Race was designed to keep us all in our place –
skin tone, hair texture,
    genetic features on your face.
A categorisation of our physical condition –
the race for life is a competition.

First World, Third World
and those in between.
Do you see how it equates?
Do you understand what I mean?

A race is never just the path ahead –
politics and economics play their parts
    that's dread.
How do we justify this inequality?
We can't – it's an impossibility.

Racist competitions corrupt the game,
designed without morality, conscience or shame.
First place, second place,
    third place will always remain –
gold, silver or bronze – who do we blame?

The true meaning of life
    transcends the concept of race.
No one will ever win or assume the real first place.
Inequalities, injustice and outlandish demands
were built with the lust of greedy men's hands.

Those same hands should reach out
to spread compassion and erase the doubt,
because this world is not yours or mine –
as humans, our existence is living
    on borrowed time.

FIGHTING FOR PEACE

Like a baby, Liverpool struggled
to stand on her own two feet.
The Great War was over – supplies were sparse
and there was rationing on food to eat.

The fog and the smog were unwelcomed guests
that added to the doom and gloom.
Austerity and depression
    occupied Upper Pit Street
so Parliament Street is where black people
    found room.

Leaving behind their place of birth
    to reside in the motherland –
seeking to find a better life,
    so they ventured to England
to make a contribution –
    that's what these black men had in mind,
but equality and justice these black men
    could not find.

Duke Street was removed from the poverty
that dwelt on Mill Street in Liverpool Eight.
Princes Avenue, Newton and Beauford Street
were places where black and white
    would copulate.

Black servicemen fought on the battleground –
a fearless heart pounding in their chest.
Discrimination, segregation, misconception
divorced the black population from the rest.

It was out of the frying pan into the fire –
the battle was now on Liverpool's streets.
Liverpool was hostile, in fact very vile,
and the black man had to retreat.

Pleading to the Lord Mayor got them nowhere
as their cries fell on deaf ears.
The Lord Mayor made a radical decision,
yes discrimination to alleviate his citizens' fears.

When the locals made outrageous claims,
    shouting racist names –
tensions exploded as the battles increased.
Black men had fought in the Great War
    and didn't want to fight no more
but were ready and prepared to fight for PEACE.

THE WAR CONTINUES

After the metal curtains of war were fully drawn,
the fabric of the landscape was distorted and torn.
Like ants the troops retreated
    from the burning embers,
but justice and liberty did not await black soldiers.

Now back in Liverpool they had to fight
    to survive –
they had fought for king and country
    and were still alive.
Returning to the loved ones they had left behind,
there was no hero's welcome –
    love was hard to find.

They thought the war was over,
    but they faced a whole new plight.
The racism in Liverpool was so severe
    they became prisoners at night.
Now deemed as social lepers,
    they had very little support –
they were treated like slaves
    who were sold and bought.

The murder of Charles Wooton 1919
    turned the city into one of flames
as the powers-that-be hid their faces
    with a cloak of shame.
The church and the state didn't have a clue
    to a solution –
a mindset of prejudice added fuel
    to the devastation.
The Lord Mayor stepped forward
    with an astute suggestion,
'The answer is simple and clear –
    the answer is repatriation.'
I think to myself, it seems peculiar,
    yes very strange –
in the grand scheme of things
    very little has changed.

Immigration is still an issue,
    as it was then back in the day –
not all black soldiers who fought for Britain
    have the right of stay.
Many have lobbied parliament,
    but their efforts were in vain
as some of them have been repatriated
    back to from where they came.

If you go to battle for Britain
    and your skin is black –
make sure you know who the real enemy is
    before you attack.
When you settle back into your civvies,
    you will still face flack
by the same flag you were defending –
    Britain's Union Jack.

A LETTER OF CONCERN

*The Town Hall,
Liverpool,
13th May 1919*

Dear Home Secretary in Parliament London,
I am writing this letter to you.
I have had a visit from the Ethiopian Association –
I need your advice on what to do.

Six hundred African-British subjects
are stranded here in the city of Liverpool.
They are anxious to return home to Africa
as their treatment in the city by the locals
    is tantamount to cruel.

Though many of them have served
    in our armed forces,
they have strange practices,
    not to mention their culture.
Many have married British women
    and have children –
some say the races should not mix,
    they find this practice vulgar.

Speaking for myself, I would just like to say
this is not the way I think –
but if this situation is not resolved soon,
our city will soon be on the brink.
Companies won't employ coloured men,
as employers and the trade unions conspire
to up hold segregation in the work place –
integration is not what they desire.

I am caught in the middle –
    which way should I turn?
I say – pay them five pounds
    and then repatriate them.
It's a small sum to pay for their return,
to relieve us of this Black irritation problem.

Can you give my concern your urgent attention?
I beg your haste in dealing with this matter –
these coloured men bring out the worst
    in our men.
These black men are destroying our culture.

I am, Sir, your obedient servant,
John Ritchie, Lord Mayor.

P.S. Our city would once again be light,
    bright and all right!
    And did I mention – all white.

FALLING TEARS

I looked into the distance
as I sat along the shore.
The horizon was blood orange
my thoughts were deep, clear but raw.

In my head I saw a picture,
very clear to see –
a ship on the ocean
heading towards me.

My eyes squinted
as I looked across the shore and all.
An overwhelming feeling took hold
as my tears started to fall.

Vivid was the vision
before my very eyes –
harbouring bad intentions
of stealing land and skies.

A ship so huge with sails and masts –
cannons loaded ready to blast.
St. George's Cross blood red and bold,
as history will soon unfold.

I sensed my ancestors encompassing me –
spiritually aware, roaming happy and free,
did not anticipate their fate
creeping in from the sea.

The fruit was in abundance –
the land flourished so divine.
Just a moment in history
would forever change their lives and mine.

Their feet firmly placed in the sand –
this was their home,
this was their land.
Pride and respect stood hand in hand.

Adorning their necks, hands and feet
were cowry shells for luck so sweet –
but very soon to be replaced
with chains of iron and steel encased.

Disembarking from their ships
the sweat beads on their face –
no compassion for humanity,
only brutality and disgrace.

Causing fear, anguish and pain –
invasion took hold amidst the strain,
separating a child from the arms of its mother,

a father and son, sister and brother.
Economics was the driver
on this haunting ride.
Your strategy was clear –
to conquer and divide.

Expanding your empire
for influence and power –
world domination was your aim
from the top of your ivory tower.

Why do you feel you're better
than my rich ancestry –
brutally crushing their identity
with your illusion of cultural superiority?

That day I wept like no tomorrow –
my heart was filled with pain and sorrow
The fear, the pain of this history –
and still not one single apology.

HOPE

HOPE....
is a well travelled road
when despair and distress colours our view.

HOPE....
binds us together
like the ingredient of a nourishing pepper-pot stew.

HOPE....
is the heartbeat
composing a rhythm across the generations.

HOPE....
is the jewel in the crown,
the salvation of all nations.

HOPE....
is resilient and tenacious –
the substance of the things we all need.

HOPE....
is a state of mind –
embrace HOPE as a means to succeed.

HOPE....
is the driving force,
inspiring right from the very start.

HOPE....
is an immense journey –
WALK WITH HOPE IN YOUR HEART.

TIME

Life giver
History maker
Eternal dealer
Great healer
Punctual master
Invaluable teacher
Infinite promoter
Moment seizer
Season greeter
Tempo meter
Minute drainer
Money gainer
Final hour
Present power
Clock components
Fleeting moments

A CITY FIT TO LIVE IN

SHE IS A CITY FIT TO LIVE IN –
SHE'S IN A HEALTHY PLACE TO BE.
YOU'LL NEVER WALK ALONE
WITH A DOSE OF SCOUSE HOSPITALITY.
SHE IS A CITY THAT IS THRIVING –
SHE'S GOT A TICKET TO RIDE.
SHE IS A CITY UNIQUE IN MANY WAYS –
LIVERPOOL ON MERSEYSIDE.

A Royal Charter was granted
    in Twelve Hundred and Seven
and ever since that time
    Liverpool has been driven.
European Capital City of Culture
    in Two Thousand and Eight –
this was an invitation to the world
    to come and celebrate.
A city steeped in history, a city known worldwide –
you brought wealth and prosperity to Britannia
    beyond Merseyside.
In the Trans-Atlantic Slave Trade
    you played a major part –
you were the main blood vessel
    pumping the wealth into Britain's heart.

A chapter of brutality
    like the world has never seen –
trading in cotton, sugar, rum, tobacco
    and also human beings.
A Maritime City – you were a major seaport
where merchants became filthy rich
    with the goods they sold and bought.
So the foundation was established,
    the merchants they were paid,
Liverpool became "The Pool of Life".
    Yes!!! Liverpool was made.
Now Liverpool is standing tall
    for all the world to see –
a city rich in heritage and culture –
    Yes! The World in One City.

SHE IS A CITY FIT TO LIVE IN –
SHE'S IN A HEALTHY PLACE TO BE.
YOU'LL NEVER WALK ALONE
WITH A DOSE OF SCOUSE HOSPITALITY.
SHE IS A CITY THAT IS THRIVING –
SHE'S GOT A TICKET TO RIDE.
SHE IS A CITY UNIQUE IN MANY WAYS –
LIVERPOOL ON MERSEYSIDE.

Now Scouse is an identity in name,
    character and culture.
Scousers are known across the land
for their language, dish and their nature.
Europe's oldest Black community
    and oldest Chinese community too.
The largest Irish community outside Dublin
    completes our cultural stew.
The Sixties was a magical time
    when Liverpool was rocking.
Our talent shone in the limelight and fame
    just kept on knocking.
Comedians, writers and actors –
    we've got them by the score;
an adventurous city that speaks its mind –
    you couldn't ask for anything more.
Then the dread time came
    which served to dim your flame –
they said it was unemployment,
    militants and riots that tarnished your name.
The Hillsborough disaster struck
    like a major heart attack.
Finally justice was served
    and so the city bounced back –
now you are a World Heritage Site
    in the company of a select few.
You rose like a phoenix from the ashes,
    because that's what Scousers do.

Creativity is our forte –
> medicine for the mind, body and soul.

We have a passion that burns like fire –
> we inspire, that's our goal.

SHE IS A CITY FIT TO LIVE IN –
SHE'S IN A HEALTHY PLACE TO BE.
YOU'LL NEVER WALK ALONE
WITH A DOSE OF SCOUSE HOSPITALITY.
SHE IS A CITY THAT IS THRIVING –
SHE'S GOT A TICKET TO RIDE.
SHE IS A CITY UNIQUE IN MANY WAYS –
LIVERPOOL ON MERSEYSIDE.

We have world-renowned bands,
> entertainers and the sounds of Merseybeat.

We also have two cathedrals
> that adorn Hope Street –

our famous Liver Birds
> which are perched on the Liver Clocks,

the Adelphi Hotel, St. George's Hall,
> the King's and Albert Docks.

At football we are outstanding
> in the way we play the game –

Liverpool FC and Everton FC have success
> as their middle name.

Our galleries, museums and theatres
> all take centre stage –

Central Library with its technology
    takes the city into a brand-new age.
Sail the ferry across the River Mersey,
    checkout the famous skyline –
get a classical treat at the Philharmonic Hall,
    the experience is sublime.
The Grand National, LIMF, Africa Oye,
    Positive Vibration and WOW –
if you feel like you need some retail therapy,
    you can shop at Liverpool One now.
A film set for LA Productions television dramas,
    movies and documentaries,
the SuperLambanana, the Shanghai Arch,
    parks, LIPA and Universities.
So I'm calling BBC Radio Merseyside
    and Radio City to air a view or two –
just to say You'll Never Walk Alone
    in My Liverpool Home.
That's why Liverpool *I love you* –
    Yes! Liverpool, *we love you!!!*

R LIVERPOOL

R LIVERPOOL
is me Ma an me Da,
'Hiya' an 'Tarah' –
du know wha a mean laaaaa.

R LIVERPOOL
is me little sister Pippy –
she puts on lippy
before she goes the chippy.

R LIVERPOOL
is me Ma is a Blue,
me Da is a Red.
De both got wed,
share de same bed –
now get dat round yer head.

R LIVERPOOL
is 'Hey love R yer dancing?'
'Why who's askin?'
'I want wedding bells an romancing,
erotic multi-taskin –
dat's why am askin.'

R LIVERPOOL
is when things get heavy,
we go for a bevvy
wid R kid Eddie –
we make the ship steady.

R LIVERPOOL
is da natural Scouse flow –
so when we go toe to toe
we always steal de show.
We do doe don't we doe.

R LIVERPOOL
is some parents at the school gates
in satin pyjamas with a little flare –
trout pout an slap on, an rollers in their hair.
Yer see dem when yer out shoppin –
yer see dem everywhere.

R LIVERPOOL
is some say we can't get a job.
De say we go out on the rob –
shut yer stupid little gob,
yer silly little knob.

R LIVERPOOL
is comedy, culture, sport an a famous stew –
two cathedrals, two Liverbirds
    an a Lambanana or two,
the River Mersey where the ferry sails.
We're Scouse, we're resilient, as hard as nails.

R LIVERPOOL
is Tocky, Kenni, Anfield an Allertun,
Speke, Aigburth, Old Swan an Evertun –
West Derby, Broad Green,
    Knotty Ash and Garstun,
Kirkby, Fazakerley, Wavertree an Wooltun.
An if a didn't mention your part of town –
don't do yer nut.
Calm down, calm down.

R LIVERPOOL
is you an me, us an we –
de World in One City,
a multi-cultural identity.
This Pool of Life is known globally.
Yes, R Liverpool is whatever yer want it to be –
because IT'S R LIVERPOOL.

LFC POETRY IN MOTION

WE ARE LIVERPOOL– LISTEN TO THE ROAR.
WE ARE LIVERPOOL – THIS MEANS MORE.

Take a look around the Albert Dock –
see the Liver Birds and the Liver Clocks.
Sail the ferry across the Mersey –
with a famous skyline steeped in history.
Two cathedrals adorn Hope Street –
The Baltic Quarter, The Cavern, Mersey Beat.
European Capital City of Culture –
    known world-wide.
We are Liverpool with a 'Ticket to Ride'.

On the other side of town,
green velvet turf laid on the mound.
Fortress Anfield, hallowed ground –
a football shrine, we wear the crown.
Kopites flood through the gates –
special nights we celebrate.
LFC – cream of the crop –
anthems ring out from the Kop.

L - I - V - E - R - P double O - L
LIVERPOOL FC.

Whilst the REDS were ripping teams apart,
fans walked with hope in their heart.
Shankly, Paisley, Fagan, Dalglish –
football excellence, Europe's elite.
The Liver Bird, the Liverpool crest –
LFC wear the colours of success.
The 70s and 80s – total domination.
Every season a cause for celebration.

King Kenny, John Barnes, Ian Rush Supreme –
winning multiple trophies, an outstanding team.
Hysel, Hillsborough, disaster and pain.
Justice for the 96 – here we come again.
Since the 1990s it's hard to believe –
thirty years since we won the league.
Suarez, Torres, Stevie G –
Carragher, Houllier, Rafa, one family.

Do you remember the time the team slipped up?
I couldn't believe we didn't win a cup.
Then the Normal One hit the scene –
'In Klopp We Trust' fulfilling dreams.
Salah, Mane, Trent, Firmino –
Ali, Millie, Van Dijk, Captain Hendo.
Heavy Metal football blowing teams away –
we are Liverpool, that's the way we play.

Allez, Allez, Allez, Allez, Allez, Allez.

Champions of Europe, Champions of the World.
This is our story – watch as it unfurls.
Home and Away we're dynamite.
We have won the Premier League Title –
    the future is bright.
Poetry in Motion – we are Liverpool.
Poetry in Motion – we are Liver 'cool'.
Poetry in Motion –
we have brought the Premier League title home.
WE ARE LIVERPOOL –
    YOU'LL NEVER WALK ALONE!

BRILLIANT BOBBY FIRMINO

SI SENOR –
GIVE THE BALL TO BOBBY
    AND HE WILL SCORE.
SI SENOR –
BOBBY YOU'RE THE ONE THE FANS ADORE.

Samba magic, LFC's number Nine –
an amazing talent with a dazzling smile,
supersonic silky skills so sublime.
A dribbling master class with grace and style –
an immense work rate
    when the REDS are cooking,
a plethora of goals, yeah without even looking.
Bobby Dazzler assists – backheels galore,
Kung Fu kick celebrations and the matador
spearheading the front three, impacting the score.
All around the ground, fans sing *Si Senor.*
Brazilian brilliance always ready to erupt –
bagging the winning goal v Flamengo
    to win the Club World Cup.
Scoring a last-minute winner against PSG –
in the UCL your goal knocked out
    Manchester City.
I remember the screamer you scored
    against Stoke –
it was a rocket, hitting the net in a trail of smoke.

A hat-trick v Arsenal left defenders on their bum –
that Sunday afternoon Bobby was having fun.
Your last goal at Anfield scored against
    Aston Villa –
your last goal for the REDS
    was in a four-four thriller.
362 matches, 111 goals plus those 79 assists –
your Brazilian magic, we the fans will truly miss.
Seven major trophies won with Liverpool FC –
a legend, an icon, recognised globally.
Fortress Anfield was the place
    where you made your name –
on that hallowed ground, you played
    the beautiful game.
Now that you are leaving,
    we the fans will feel the pain –
but our honour and respect for you
    will always remain.

As we bid you farewell, with love in our heart,
we wish you all the best Bobby
    in your fresh new start.
Your spirit will always remain
    in our Liverpool home –
our hero Roberto Magic Firmino –
    You'll Never Walk Alone.

SI SENOR –
GIVE THE BALL TO BOBBY
   AND HE WILL SCORE.
SI SENOR –
BOBBY YOU'RE THE ONE THE FANS ADORE.

HEARTFELT LOVE

My love for you a heartfelt expression –
deep in emotion, deeper in passion.
The ocean's depth seems so small –
the highest mountain not so tall.

I stand by you whether we rise or fall –
riding on Cloud Nine, or backs against the wall.
There's nothing that I wouldn't do for you
to prove to you my love is true.

To kiss your lips, caress your face –
to sooth your soul, make your heart race.
You are my world, my only treasure –
a treasure so rare and beyond measure.

I cherish the day our love story started.
I can't imagine us ever being parted.
I'm right by your side – together we're strong.
I celebrate that our love has lasted so long.

BEAUTIFULLY BLISS

When times are blue and life is a trial –
my mission in life is to make you smile.

With love, laughter, hugs and kisses,
a warm embrace, heartfelt wishes
to alleviate your stress and strain –
to free you from your hurt and pain.

Close to my heart, wrapped in my arms –
channelling my love to sooth and calm.
Ears always open when you need to speak –
I'm your strength when you're feeling weak.

To raise your spirit, ignite your body and mind
with a cohesive force that truly binds.
From a sensual place way deep inside,
we sparkle and shine when our spirits collide.

Know you are loved, whether near or far –
truly loved for who you are.
Life with you is so beautiful and bliss –
I'm sending a great big hug and a massive kiss.

YOU MAKE MY LIFE WORTHWHILE

The twinkle in your eyes,
the sparkle of your smile,
the sassiness of your spirit –
you make my life worthwhile.

The beauty of your face –
always oozing grace and style.
Your very presence lights up my world –
you make my life worthwhile.

For your love and sweet caress,
I would walk a million miles.
A beautiful flower in this garden of life –
you make my life worthwhile.

Your kindness, your humanity,
flow like the River Nile.
You are invaluable, a precious gem –
you make my life worthwhile.

To prove my love to you,
I would wrestle with a crocodile,
sleep on red hot coals, on a bed of nails –
you make my life worthwhile.

A natural woman, genuine and real –
no pretence or fake profile.
The love we have is eternal –
you make my life worthwhile.

Tenacious in your endeavours,
stepping out with a rainbow smile,
driven and inspirational –
you make my life worthwhile.

A woman of distinction,
phenomenal and versatile,
I know we were made for each other –
you make my life worthwhile.

LOVE LIFE LAUGHTER

Love, life and laughter –
that's what everyone is after.
There's no need to live with sorrow and pain –
no-one wants to live their life in vain.
Let's create a foundation that is firm and positive –
life is not just survival, it's a right to live.
Look deep within yourself
    with what you can give –
don't player-hate, don't be negative.
Make a conscious contribution
    that you know will last –
your recognition will serve the future,
    present and past.
So keep the fires burning, be direct –
embrace the human condition with full effect.
Selfishness is a bitter pill for our collective health –
seek spiritual values, not material wealth.
Unity is the medicine we all need to heal –
then love, life and laughter can be yours for real.

WHEN IT COMES TO LOVING

Picture an island
where the sunshine feels so sweet,
and the trees bear tropical fruits
to the rhythm of a reggae beat.
A fisherman casts his net
in the midst of the deep blue sea,
while a stranger observes his life
from the shores of a foreign country.

The stranger had a plan to control the man,
his situation upon the island.
That's not right – he'll have to fight,
he'll have to fight for his human rights.

See when it comes to loving,
they don't want to give.
And when it comes to life,
they don't know how to live.
The teachings they give us
they are negative,
when all we are fighting for
is strictly positive.

We have to fight, fight for what's right.
We have to fight, fight with all our might.

Look how the sun brightens up the day –
the stranger's presence fades it away.
The island turns to cold concrete –
the stranger's plan is filled with deceit.

Now check out the city
designed from cold concrete –
furnished in luxury,
people jammin on the uptown street.
A rich man plays his tune
and it rocks the whole nation.
They think it is safety,
but the reality is destruction.

The stranger had a plan to control the man,
his situation upon the island.
That's not right – he'll have to fight,
he'll have to fight to keep his future bright.

See when it comes to loving,
they don't want to give.
And when it comes to life,
they don't know how to live.
The teachings they give us
they are negative,
when all we are fighting for
is strictly positive.

We have to fight, fight for what's right.
We have to fight, fight with all our might.
We will have to fight, fight to ease our plight.
We will have to fight, fight to retain our light.

CAN YOU FEEL IT

CAN YOU FEEL IT –
CAN YOU FEEL YOUR SPIRIT MOVING?
CAN YOU FEEL IT –
CAN YOU FEEL YOUR SPIRIT GROOVING?

We play reggae music day and night –
we play this music to shed forth some light.
So, everybody inna this session –
you have to groove to this roots vibration.
Some try to tell us that we are different –
but I know that is propaganda,
cause when I man check creation
I know there's only the one creator.

CAN YOU FEEL IT –
CAN YOU FEEL YOUR SPIRIT MOVING?
CAN YOU FEEL IT –
CAN YOU FEEL YOUR SPIRIT GROOVING?

People we should come together
and put away small differences,
cause now it's time for loving each other –
no more ism or schism,
no more war, no more trouble.
It's time to overcome the struggle,
cause there's no need to fuss and fight –
this is the night we should all unite.

CAN YOU FEEL IT –
CAN YOU FEEL YOUR SPIRIT MOVING?
CAN YOU FEEL IT –
CAN YOU FEEL YOUR SPIRIT GROOVING?

Let the rhythm liberate your soul –
free up your mind, it's time to take control.
Live for each other, do what is right –
let harmony be your guiding light.
Fussing and fighting, war is not the answer –
divide and conquer will lead to disaster.
Music is the key, let the rhythm play –
this yah reggae vibes come to lead the way.

CAN YOU FEEL IT –
CAN YOU FEEL YOUR SPIRIT MOVING?
CAN YOU FEEL IT –
CAN YOU FEEL YOUR SPIRIT GROOVING?

MAKE THINGS HAPPEN

There are multitudes of people
    in this garden of life –
people of all persuasions,
    there are many different types.
There are those who make things happen –
    those who pioneer.
There are those who innovate –
    their talents they will share.
There are those who create –
    they are a credit to us all.
There are giants in our society –
    they are mighty and stand tall.
We need these types of people –
    leaders who lead the way.
Honour, respect and trust them –
    so long as they don't lead you astray.

There are those who watch things happen –
    they sit on the sideline.
They want to do, but wait for you –
    they do it all the time.
They hesitate and procrastinate –
    they want to get involved.
They need the motivation
    to get the problem solved.

Don't just watch things happen –
    get proactive, get things done.
Be independent not dependent –
    make your mark and be someone.
With your life be creative –
    put your words and deeds into action.
Do not be the problem –
    now go and be the solution.

Now some are problematic –
    they just didn't have a clue.
Their heads are firmly in the clouds –
    raining problems down on you.
They don't take the initiative
    to do what they should do –
a lack of imagination, no dreams to pursue.
A dose of inactivity – that's what set them back.
A vision of reality – that is what they lack.
So for the sake of humanity,
    let's pull each other through.
Make things happen in this garden of life –
then you will know the true meaning of you.

WATER

Sky drencher
Thirst quencher
Glass filler
Pool dweller
Liquid matter
Beach caresser
Fun maker
Life taker
Free runner
Perfect cleanser
Life giver
Flowing river
Lacking colour
Lacking odour
Wet in nature
World treasure

WE NEED A SOLUTION

POLLUTION, POLLUTION –
    WE NEED A SOLUTION.
POLLUTION, POLLUTION –
    WE NEED ONE NOW.
POLLUTION, POLLUTION –
    LET'S FIND A SOLUTION.
POLLUTION, POLLUTION –
    ANY WAY, ANY HOW!

Mother Earth nurtures, Mother Nature feeds –
providing all species with the things we all need.
But humans are attacking her at a rapid speed –
it's all about control and power
    fuelled by vanity and greed.
Tearing up the earth's flesh, spreading disease –
poisoning her rivers and deforesting her trees,
raising her temperatures by many degrees.
Many Island Nations are disappearing
    under the seas.

POLLUTION, POLLUTION –
    WE NEED A SOLUTION.
POLLUTION, POLLUTION –
    WE NEED ONE NOW.
POLLUTION, POLLUTION –
    LET'S FIND A SOLUTION.

POLLUTION, POLLUTION –
    ANY WAY, ANY HOW!

Marine life so wonderful diverse and exotic,
now being destroyed by humans
    dumping waste made of plastic.
Beautiful coastlines littered with rubbish
    which turns toxic,
annihilating the eco-system –
    I don't understand the logic.
For centuries factories have been
    bellowing out smoke –
now you're blaming cows farting in a field,
    is this a joke?
Air pollution, climate change –
    tell me who's at fault.
We need to find a solution–
    this situation needs to halt.

POLLUTION, POLLUTION –
    WE NEED A SOLUTION.
POLLUTION, POLLUTION –
    WE NEED ONE NOW.
POLLUTION, POLLUTION –
    LET'S FIND A SOLUTION.
POLLUTION, POLLUTION –
    ANY WAY, ANY HOW!

Preserving keystone species,
    preserving biodiversity,
keeps Mother Nature happy,
    keeps Mother Earth healthy.
Recycle and regenerate – those are the keys
for a brighter tomorrow,
    for future generations' longevity.
The solution needs to be sincere,
    coming straight from the heart –
meaning people from around the globe
    get proactive, play your part.
Act locally, think globally to alleviate this problem.
Humans – the power is in your hands,
work hard go forth and solve them.

POLLUTION, POLLUTION –
    WE NEED A SOLUTION.
POLLUTION, POLLUTION –
    WE NEED ONE NOW.
POLLUTION, POLLUTION –
    LET'S FIND A SOLUTION.
POLLUTION, POLLUTION –
    ANY WAY, ANY HOW!

SEFTON'S WONDEROUS WATERWAYS

Alongside the emerald green banks,
the murky Sefton Canal flows.
Take the bait as adventure awaits –
our journey begins, your excitement grows.

From ancient times, this wonderland
flowing from Liverpool to Leeds,
transporting coal, cotton,
    wheat, potatoes and timber –
supplying many communities' needs.

The hustle and bustle of these waterways
of the Bootle, Netherton
    and Litherland communities –
horse-drawn carts, narrow-boats,
    barges and canoes
create a hub of endless activities.

A staircase of locks links the docks,
elevates and helps the canal to thrive.
Bridges like ribs crossing the snaking waters –
blue skies, sunshine, feeling free and alive.

Escape through the gates of nature,
with aquatic damp scents, flora and fresh air.
Swans, ducks, geese, coots,

squirrels, rats, otters, water voles –
you will see them all thriving right here.

Anglers, cyclists, joggers and dog walkers
respect the grey stony towpath.
Sipping beer, BBQs and outdoor sports –
residents stroll to a rhythm whilst having a laugh.

Innovation, conservation and regeneration –
developing a legacy for the future,
creating a clean, safe environment,
preserving local traditions and culture.

Tranquility now runs throughout this place,
like lifelines running through our veins.
A place to reflect –
     a serene and comforting space,
that you will want to visit again and again.

A SYMPHONY OF COLOURS

A painting hangs in the Tate Gallery,
with bright bold colours for all to see.
The colours compose a symphony
of instruments playing in harmony.
A magical musical mystery,
now part of our history.
A rich cultural legacy
that takes us on a poetic journey.

The paint brush transforms into magic wand.
Strokes of oil on canvas take us far beyond –
a world of adventure, a world of dreams,
a world of wonder and musical themes.

Feast your eyes on tones of **GREEN** –
a velvet soft world, pure and clean.
A place where nature reigns supreme –
the musical tones are so serene.
The rhythm of life takes control –
let the music guide your soul.
Embrace the movement, enjoy the ride –
no need to run, no need to hide.

Feast your eyes on tones of **AMBER** –
with a tropical feel, a Creole culture,
where reggae and calypso
    mingle in the cool breeze
with sun-kissed beaches and tropical trees.
A Caribbean tradition and carnival sounds,
rainbow smiles beaming all around.
People are jammin, enjoying the vibe –
one love, one heart keeping the music alive.

Feast your eyes on tones of **RED** –
filled with awe, filled with dread.
The music takes on a vicious tone
which chills your body down to the bone.

As horror fills the atmosphere
your heart starts pounding, filled with fear.
You try to run, you try to escape
as the music covers the whole landscape.

Feast your eyes on tones of **BLUE** –
electric, aqua, turquoise too.
A downbeat rhythm telling the news –
the storytelling of the Blues.
Step on board, there's nothing to lose –
let the music take you on a cruise.
Sail the ocean's avenues –
discover the sounds of Rhythm and Blues.

Feast your eyes on tones of **GREY** –
Heavy Metal Rock Music, hear it play.
The beat pulsates, the world starts to shake –
Heavy Metal Rock, a musical earthquake.
The world is now electrified –
turn up the amp, it's amplified.
Neon lights illuminate the stage –
a musical explosion, musical rage.

Feast your eyes on **ORANGE** and **BROWN** –
see the sounds of jazz colour the town
with a jazzy vibe and a jazzy feel,
a jazzy bass line keeping things jazzy real,
a jazzy scat and jazzy moves,
a jazzy dance with a jazzy groove,
a jazzy drum, a jazzy smile,
a zoot suit with a jazzy style.

Feast your eyes on **BLACK** and **WHITE** –
contrasting sounds that unite.
Piano keys tinkle and excite –
music to our ears, sheer delight.
An orchestral crescendo signals the end –
music and art are now the best of friends.
An extraordinary journey, an amazing feat –
a journey well travelled,
    our journey now complete.

BOOK

Library dweller
Shelf decorator
Paper pleaser
Chapter teaser
Great storyteller
Cover compeller
Knowledge feeder
Information breeder
Emotional choker
Physical tearjerker
Tale weaver
Dream believer
Image narrator
Verbal creator
Late night burner
Page turner

WILL OUR GRANDCHILDREN BE ROBOTIC?

Will our grandchildren be robotic?
That's the million-dollar question, a very hot topic.
With no feelings or emotions,
    will they be automatic?
Will it spread throughout the land
    like an epidemic?

Will our grandchildren
continue to communicate –
be able to hold a debate
about world affairs and its terrible state?

Will our grandchildren
come to realise
they're being dehumanised
in a world that is more mechanised?

Will our grandchildren
lose all contact with nature
to a technological culture
with a virtual future?

Will our grandchildren
become more paranoid
by becoming more android,
becoming less and less humanoid?

We have designer clothes for the designer lady.
You can design your face –
    some have gone designer crazy.
Are we designing a monster?
    Well some say maybe!
Choose the colour of the eyes
    of your designer baby.

Will we fall for cloning and genetic engineering?
Are we creating grandkids
    that are really uncaring?
Who have no idea what a raw potato looks like –
the only things they recognise are symbols
    like Disney and Nike.

Are we reproducing grandkids
    that don't go out to play?
Whose only function is to sit in front
    of a computer night and day?
Are we reproducing grandkids
    that don't know how to cook –
with low self esteem and a grim outlook?

Well you can log on eBay and resister a bid –
yes get on-line and spend a few quid.
You can buy anything including a cyber grandkid –
if it doesn't work out, you can always get rid.

So will our grandchildren be robotic?
Well, they are changing as we speak.
They're starting a new race in cyber space –
there is one being born every week.

IT'S WHERE WE'RE GOING

We know the past – we call it history.
We've seen the shame and the dignity.
The future is one big mystery –
now it's time to shape our destiny.

We know ourselves – we are the fruit.
We develop and grow straight from the roots.
In this garden of life we seek out the truth.
Give us the real deal, cause there's no substitute

Nature gave birth and we received her law.
The garden was tranquil until Man went to war.
Now they've developed technology
    like you've never seen before.
Now we're looking to the future
    to see what is in store.

Some have no faith – some practice religion.
Some study the sciences,
    while some are on a mission.
Some have great ideas,
    whist some have no vision.
Some haven't got a clue –
    some are making a decision.

So we roam this creation in the hope of peace.
We pray to God for the violence to cease.
Let equality and justice be the centrepiece –
with unity in the community, the love will increase.
We have come from a place
    that is fruitful and green –
but we're destroying the garden
    with a monster of a machine.
We have to change our ways –
    we got to come clean.
It's where we are going that is important,
    if you know what I mean.

BEING HUMAN

A chair has legs, but a chair can't walk.
A river has a mouth, but a river can't talk.
A potato has eyes, but it can't shed a tear.
A mountain has 'ears', but a mountain can't hear.
A clock has hands, but a clock can't clap.
A shoe has a tongue, but it can't taste or rap.
A glass has a lip, but the glass can't pout.
The wind can whistle,
>but the wind doesn't have a mouth.

A bottle has a neck, but it doesn't wear a tie.
A car has wings, but a car can't fly.
A book has spine, but a book can't bend.
A lettuce has a heart,
>but it can't love you like a friend.

A comb has teeth, but a comb can't bite.
A watch has fingers, but it can't switch off the light.
A storm has an eye, but the storm can't see.
Poetry has many moods and tones,
>just like you and me –

THE HUMAN FAMILY!

ACKNOWLEDGEMENTS

I would like to extend my heartfelt thanks to all who commissioned me to write some of the poems in this collection. Your trust in my work and creativity to bring your visions, emotions and stories to life has inspired me to deliver poetry that captures your sentiments lyrically, allowing them to come to life and flourish. I am honoured to have contributed to your projects.

Equally as significant are all my readers, supporters, and those who have inspired or encouraged me along the way. Your belief in my work has been a humbling experience.
This book is not just my book – it's our book.

LEVI TAFARI

NOTES

A City Fit To Live In

Commissioned by Health Systems Global, an organisation of public health researchers, policymakers, and practitioners worldwide. The poem served as the opening for their 2018 biennial conference in Liverpool, welcoming delegates and showcasing the diversity within the city.

Letter of Concern, Fighting for Peace and The War Continues

A trio of poems commissioned by Writing on the Wall (WOW) in preparation for the 2015 centenary of the First World War. The brief given to me was to focus on the plight of people from Black Commonwealth countries who were left stranded and impoverished in Liverpool with no way of getting home once the war had ended.

A Symphony of Colours

Commissioned by Tate Liverpool, August 2020 for their project Tate Stories. Ten paintings were put to a number of poets including myself. We were asked to choose a painting and describe it poetically, after which we were given details of the artist and the painting. Ironically, the painting I had chosen was by a Jamaican artist – which I did not know at the time. I had been instantly drawn in by the colours and the vibrancy, enabling the lyrics to flow naturally.

Acts of Kindness

Commissioned by BBC Radio Merseyside, May 2020 during Covid Lockdown, to capture the kindness, generosity and support we gave one another during this testing period.

Brilliant Bobby Firmino

Commissioned by Red Men TV, June 2023 to highlight and celebrate the skill and achievements of the Liverpool forward and midfielder. It would also to be used as part of a TV documentary.

Let us Celebr8

The late Benjamin Zephaniah recommended me for a government funded initiative in 2006. The brief was to write a poem which emphasises embracing diversity, rejecting discrimination, and fostering unity. It celebrates differences in race, gender, religion, sexuality, ability, and humanity – advocating respect, inclusion, and shared coexistence. Such is the success of this poem that it has been used across all sectors and disciplines and most recently as the relaunch of Spellow Library in 2025.

LFC Poetry in Motion

Commissioned by Live Wire Sport, March 2020, on behalf of the English Football Premier League to celebrate Liverpool FC being crowned the Premier League champions. The poem was also used for the EFPL international media campaign in various platforms.

Sefton Wondrous Waterways

The Poetry Society in conjunction with Sefton Canal and River Trust Northwest commissioned me to write a poem in May 2022 for the launch of the regeneration of Sefton canals. Plaques of each verse of the poem were erected along the bank of the Sefton Canal.

Anchored and **Shifting**

Bisakah Saker, Director of Chaturangan Dance Company commissioned me to write 6 poems for the *Sacred Moves* project in 2004 – which highlighted the experiences and challenges of the immigration and migration of people. These were also part of a successful UK tour.